How To Make Money At A Garage Sale

What Do I Have & What Is It Worth?

By

Natalie Johnson

Table Of Contents

Introduction

I want to thank you and congratulate you for downloading the book, *How to Make Money at a Garage Sale*.

This book contains proven steps and strategies on making money at a garage sale.

A garage sale is undoubtedly one of the best ways to get rid of stuff from your home which you no longer need anymore. A successful garage sale can yield positive outcomes. It can help you raise funds (which you could use for buying necessities) or it can unclutter your home (you'll still get a decent amount of money from it).

Beyond the desire of earning some quick money and getting rid of things that are no longer needed, what is it about garage sales that draw sellers and buyers alike? Well, here's one good answer to that – the chance to both relive and create memories.

The things you're going to sell have been part of your past; you have memories associated with them. Now, since you're selling those items, you're actually giving other people a chance to create new memories that are connected to yours. Of course, there's also the possibility that some of your customers have had memorable experiences with things identical to those you have on sale. In that sense, your temporary entrepreneurial endeavor could give them the opportunity to relive some of their most precious memories.

This book will help you create a good garage sale experience for your buyers and ultimately, yourself. It would help you accomplish the entire process like a pro – from the preparation stage, to the layout stage, and to the day-after stage. You would know about setting prices, items that are easy to get rid of, as well as tactics on how to advertise and sell.

Thanks again for downloading this book. I hope you enjoy it!

"Happiness is your own treasure because it lies within you."

-Prem Rawat

Chapter 1
Getting Started

You probably have a lot of goods you no longer use – or want. Of course, you can just throw them all away, or you can bring out the family phonebook to find out which of your cousins will be stoked to have your mid-80's video game console. But why would you call (or spam the social media pages of) distant family members when you can bring out tables and set up a store just right on the curb? Or maybe, just tidy up your old punk-rock high school band rehearsal place and set it up there? (Yes. It's the garage).

A garage sale (yard sale, basement sale, or thrift sale) is a good way not only to make a quick buck, but also an efficient technique to unclutter your house and finally give you that storage space you have always wished for. Moreover, this is a good way to raise funds if you want to help a charity. Your profit depends on what you're selling and the amount of time your sale is up. On average, yard sales in the US generate a profit of $100 to $200 a day. But if you play your cards right, you could pretty much end up with a $1,000 just for the weekend!

Before anything else, pulling off a successful garage sale is not just about placing your stuff in a big pile and letting your buyers navigate through the mountain of junk you just created. You have to put a lot of things in consideration to have a successful garage sale.

Gather together all the stuff you no longer need or want. Search all over your house (especially in the closet, attic, and garage) and look for different items that you no longer need anymore such as, clothes, gadgets, shoes, furniture – just grab anything that you can find. Gather them all and choose which items you would like to sell.

Inventory and Pricing. Once you're done gathering all your stuff, make a list of the items then set a price for each. That way, you won't have to try to come up with appropriate prices on the spot. In other words, you'll be able to avoid overpricing things. You'll also avoid the mistake of setting prices that are far too low.

Attach a price tag. Sticking a price tag on each item is surely a big help. This will help you save a lot of time and energy from answering all of the customer's questions about the price of each item.

Talk to the Local Authorities. In certain jurisdictions, a permit is required. Some cities don't require licenses or permits, so long as you have no more than one garage sale each quarter per calendar year. While in other cities, only two garage sales per year are allowed for each household group, family, or individual. Talk to someone from your town hall about this.

Many "garage sellers" commit the mistake of not taking heed the local ordinances of the town or city regarding garage sales. Most of them think that garage sales incomes are too small to attract the attention of IRS or other tax officials. They rationalize that there is no way for those officials to keep track of who are doing garage sales and how often per year. They couldn't be more wrong.

Printed and online advertisements used for garage sales could be used as evidences. Not to mention, the testimonies of neighbors, homeowner officers and even the buyers, themselves. Evading these laws could cost you more in fines and penalties compared when you actually pay the required taxes.

Depending on which state you are in, for instance in Texas, having more than 2 garage sales per year would place you in a category of operating a business. As such, you would be subjected to 6.2% income tax on all your sales (up to the last cent) plus an additional 2% on sales tax. Also, permits to hold garage sales would be required. In Oklahoma City, all garage sellers are required to obtain permits.

The Limited Sales, Excise and Use Tax states that a serial garage sale holder (more than 2 garage sales a year), has to obtain a business permit and license, pay sales tax and income tax on all profits. Plus, there are additional regulations that you need to follow or a corresponding fine or penalty would be enforced.

Be sure to talk and explain to the authorities/regulating bodies in your area if you're planning to do a garage sale. That way, you will be aware if a permit or license is necessary and if there are certain rules to follow. Know for how many days you would be allowed to sell your stuff. Find out if there are restrictions about putting up a sign for advertising. In addition, take note of what you're allowed to sell. In most instances, acquiring new merchandises for the sole purpose of reselling them is not allowed.

After confirming that you do need to get a permit, ask about the timeframes and deadlines. How many days before the actual garage sale should you be able to secure a permit. Also, ask how many days a single permit remains valid. You can check your town hall website if they provide information about garage sale permits. Some cities also allow garage sellers to apply online for permits.

Be considerate to your neighbors. You can't automatically assume that everyone will be on the same page when it comes to your "endeavor". Some people might find the amount of people visiting your neighborhood, troubling. The additional noise and traffic from all the people might bother them, so it's advisable to explain to your neighbors what's going on. Also, with a lot of people coming and going, if certain problems arise, it will be somewhat difficult to get to the bottom of things right away.

After you talk to your neighbors, it might also be ideal to ask them to join your cause. If things worked out and if people pitched in, a neighborhood sale or a community sale is really a site to see. You're not going to compete against the Highway Corridor Sale (It is the World's Longest Yard Sale with all public and private sellers spread along a 630-mile road covering five U.S. states) but it's a good way to build camaraderie in your community.

Involve your family or friends. Ask your friends or family to join you in managing the garage sale. You could try to convince them by asking them to sell some of their own stuff. Regardless of whether you believe that you're more than capable of managing the garage sale, getting help from those closest to you would surely be beneficial. Besides, it's always good to have a wider selection of items to sell.

But keep in mind that although they want to sell a few things in your garage sale, those are not yours. So, ask them to prepare their own inventory lists. Aside from that, when a buyer's asking to get someone else's item at a lower price, you shouldn't even begin to negotiate (unless you've already asked for permission to do so). That way, you'll prevent conflicts from arising (and you won't lose the trust of a friend or family member).

Choose a date and time. Most people start their sales on Friday or Saturday to fully take advantage of the coming weekend. Or, you can take advantage of the payday. Moreover, you can also check your area's big yard sale day.

Usually the busiest time of the day is around 7 or 8 in the morning until around 11 am or noon. Packing things up should probably begin at around 4 or 5 in the afternoon. If you really want to maximize your time for those latecomers, 6 pm should ultimately be your closing hour.

If you're thinking of the holidays, assuming that since there's no work people will willingly go to your neighborhood and look for some random stuff, think again. Don't schedule your garage sale on a holiday, especially on the big ones like 4th of July and Memorial Day. People will get so caught up in their personal time-off that wandering on someone else's garage will be at the bottom of their to-do list.

Setting the date could also be tricky, especially if your location is known to have different seasons. Ideally, nothing beats a summer-time garage sale. But if you want to optimize a bit more, spring should definitely come to mind. People will have that itch to go out after staying inside their houses during the cold weather. So, when they do get out, you'll have your bargains ready for them. It is also wise to check the weather forecast. You don't want to sell under the rain, right?

Look for a good spot. If you don't have an ideal area in your home, you could ask your relatives or friends for help; it's likely that they have a good place for your sale. Pick a location that is easy to get into and can easily be found. Also, think of customers with cars; as much as possible, choose a place that can accommodate people with rides. There's no need to get something with a huge parking space though. An area that can handle at least 3 to 5 cars should be enough to help boost your profit.

You should avoid areas with ongoing road construction projects or repair work. In addition, be sure not to block sidewalks or the public right-of-way. Make sure you won't cause disturbance in the flow of traffic. Think of the pedestrians well and check whether you're inconveniencing them in any way.

Advertise your upcoming sale. People won't know about your garage sale if you don't advertise. One of the most important things in this venture is to get people's attention. You should advertise your sale in advance to spread the news. You need to let the people know about the date and time of your sale and where it is going to be held. Be sure to include a list of some of your available items, especially if you have items that are very old or hard to find.

Organize your display. Be sure you have enough tables for your display. You don't have to pile your items on top of each other. Everything should be visible and wonderful to look at. You can display small things on top of the tables so they can easily be seen. Just make sure to leave enough space between tables to keep people comfortable as they inspect your items.

Large items can be placed in front of the tables to attract those passing by. Instead of folding clothes, it is best to simply hang them up so people can browse and inspect them easily. That way, you won't have to worry about folding clothes repeatedly either.

If you have electronic products, be sure to have an electrical outlet. Buyers will surely test such items, as they'd want to be sure that they are getting something in working condition. Also, prepare some trays that can be used by the buyers as shopping basket.

Have a last day deal. The last day of your garage sale is the perfect day for a massive markdown. You can offer 50% to 70% off, or go with a buy-one take-one deal. Unleash your creativity, think of good ideas for selling your leftovers.

Don't just throw your unsold items. Once you're done selling and you still have items that need to be sold, you can post your unsold things on different classified-ads websites or even on social networking sites. Some people might find your items interesting and decide to make a purchase. Of course, it's also an option to pack your leftovers and sell them in your next garage sale.

More tips to remember:
- Prepare the things/items a few days or even weeks prior to the sale.

- If not all the items are yours, ask the owners to give their items descriptions to help with the sale.
- DON'T sell anything you're not ready to say goodbye to. It's embarrassing to call a customer asking him to return the item just because you had second thoughts.
- Sharp items should be placed on sale carefully; have their edges wrapped or at least, keep them out of children's reach.
- Don't forget to check your goods not just for quality but for other things. Check the pages of books 'cause you don't know if you slipped something important in there, like a password to your account or a $100 bill.

Chapter 2

What Are Good Items to Sell?

Just as mentioned earlier, the items that have lost much of their value should be the ones on your garage sale. But before you actually begin your temporary entrepreneurial endeavor, go around your home for a bit and see what other items have served their final purpose. Your basement and attic are two good choices for beginning such a quest.

Next, check your room and the rest of your family's (if there are any) and make sure those items are indeed going to the sale. It goes without saying but just in case, only gather objects for selling and make peace with yourself that you won't see those items ever again. In other words, be sure that you won't have regrets.

You're probably thinking that different types of tools, such as power saws, drills, sets of screwdrivers, and used mowers, will have men lining up on your driveway. And the not so old beauty products, crafts, and other unusual stuff will go to the ladies. Books, cartoon hero figures, skateboards and other fun stuff are mainly for the youngsters.

Well, you'll soon find out as you open your sale that the first purchase and the customer who bought it will always shock you. Now give yourself a pat on the back after selling that holiday sweater your aunt gave to you back in '93 to someone who's the very definition of cutting-edge fashion.

With that being said, people in general will look and buy the following:

1. Antiques
These items are old and valuable, which is why potential buyers will always be curious to know the history behind them. That's why the more you know about the items you're selling—the better your chances of selling them.

Now, what qualifies as an antique? The US Customs Service defines an antique as an item with at least 100 years of age under its belt. You might be confused or perhaps even disappointed that none the objects you're looking at right now fits the qualification.

However these days, people perceive "antique" as a relative term. So, in that sense, it'd still be appropriate to say that something made during the 1950s *is* antique. If you choose to definite "antique" that way however, be sure to make it clear to your potential customers, especially to those serious about collecting relics of the past.

There is a wide array of antiques out there like clocks, toys, store signs, gas pumps, cars, figurines, watches, furniture, art, porcelain, and music boxes.

With that in mind, make sure to get a little more background info on your items. Of course, you'll also have to learn more about their value. While exploring the web would surely be useful in that pursuit, visiting pawn shops and getting involved in the antique scene are also crucial. Remember, getting a collector or a picker to purchase your antique during the garage sale is less likely to get you more money than auctioning it off.

2. Electronics (slightly broken or working but no longer state-of-the-art)

Just because you see "broken" doesn't mean you can sell a TV remote missing 70% of its buttons. This just means that there are electronics that lean a little bit to the antique-slash-collectible category.

Occasionally, you will have collectors or pickers at your doorstep and they're not just looking to buy. They are also there to make a resale and a decent profit if they see something they like which can be valuable, especially if the seller is solely selling to get more space inside the house; they won't think twice about setting up a deal and getting that thing restored.

3. Athletic Equipment

Purchasing brand new sporting equipment can be a huge blow to your budget. That's why athletic goods are a welcome category. This could be golf clubs, golf balls, cue sticks, gym bags, baseball mitts, baseball bats, football helmets, different specialty rubber shoes (basketball, running, football, tennis, soccer etc.), basketball court equipment and many more.

You could also be the one who will inspire a person to have his own gym. Selling that 3-year-old treadmill can open up a huge space in the house. Complete the experience by including dumbbells, weights, benches, mats, exercise balls, bicycles (ready-to-ride or stationary) – the list goes on.

4. Children's Clothes

If you would ask people if clothes are top sellers at a garage sale, they will probably say that you are wasting your time. Some even designate a certain spot for clothes and have everything priced a buck each— maybe even less. But it's different when it comes to children's clothes, especially the ones for babies or toddlers.

Manufacturers make adult clothes more often than baby shirts simply because kids can easily outgrow them, sometimes even in a month or two. If you still have some decent children's clothes stored somewhere in your house, you better go get them. Aside from gaining profit for something used only a few times, you'll know that several children out there will be properly clothed and you'll feel good about yourself in the process.

5. Toys

Toys differ in value depending on their condition. Better condition translates to greater bargaining power against collectors. Of course, you have to remember that at any time, kids visiting your sale can always play with your toys. If you don't want that to happen and the toy is out of its original packaging, you can make your own. Seal it so playful kids won't break it nor damage it. Needless to say, toys are very hot items at garage sales.

6. Household Appliances and Other Items

These items have the potential to be top sellers if they're all in good working condition. Dig through your garage, storage closet, cabinet drawers and honestly, don't you need a new refrigerator anyway? People will ultimately look for something they can actually use like microwaves, oven toasters, stoves, candle holders, coasters, plates, mugs, cups, novelty mugs, bowls, and sets of silverware.

7. Furniture

The people helping you will come in handy in handling these items, especially if you're selling a lot of them. Handling and moving items like beds and bookcases can be a difficult task to get around to. That's why it is advisable to ask your friends or your family to help out.

Items that fall under this category are dressers, tables, coffee tables, recliners, chairs, sofas, desks, chests, cabinets, shelves, bookcases, counters, stools, bar stools, rocking chairs, and tansu; if you have creative or novelty furniture, that would also draw potential buyers.

8. Books and Other Reading Materials

Although it depends on the available selection, books can outsell clothes (adult clothes). If you also want to clear some space in your personal library, it's definitely recommended to part with your books as well.

Bestseller paperback books will sell. If you don't have a wide selection of books, you can drop by a local book sale and buy quality ones by bulk, which you can sell for a much higher amount. Check the bestseller list or if you are an avid reader already, you probably have a good idea which types of books sell to certain demographics.

You could also include back issues of magazines with your books to offer more variety. Do not get your hopes up though; magazines can be a hit-or-miss type of item. It is wise to test them out by trying to sell them individually on the first day. If it doesn't work out, make it bargain. If you're selling them 25 cents a pop, how about selling five or even six issues for $1? Or better yet, make it a bundle instead.

If you're still making up your mind, you can't go wrong with novels and history books; a lot of people also enjoy their good mystery books. For magazines, Reader's Digest is a decent sell. While National Geographic (whichever issues they may be) will always attract a collector or even a casual buyer.

9. CDs, DVDs, Records, and Video Games

You need to make sure that all of these items are working. Test them days before you put up your sale to avoid future problems. Make sure songs don't jump when played. For game discs, see to it that you test them using at least two consoles/systems because the discs might not be the problem. Remember, consoles' lenses become defective or weak.

Check if the cases or jackets of the items are still available and in good condition. If they were, they would still be worth a lot. If the discs are scratched only from regular play, you could still sell it at a good price.

You'll be surprised at the type of the items getting sold during the big day so it would be wise to just follow your gut and sell things you think would be valuable to another person. If you have extra adaptors, AV cables, chargers, HDMI cables, drives, keychains, stamps, old coins, old calendars or any memorabilia, don't think twice and just put them on sale.

Chapter 3

How to Price Your Items

This is the part where most people who decide to have a garage sale end up spending a lot of time– pricing. What exactly is the perfect or the optimal price for every item that you have? How can you gain a decent amount of money without coming off as that one greedy guy at a garage sale?

Here are the factors to consider when pricing your items:

1. Is the item you are trying to sell currently in demand or not? Is it in or out of season? Plan your garage sale according to seasons too so that you can price them better. For instance, have the garage sale during autumn for your winter or snow stuff and equipment. Or, summer items could be priced higher when the garage sale is set during spring.

2. Is the item still in fashion? Unless the item is antique, outdated things would be valued at lower prices.

3. What is the condition of the item? Is it intact or broken? Does it have scratches? Do you still have the original packaging, (or at least, the box), or tags? In case your item still has the original tag

attached, you can price it at 70% off the marked price.

4. Are other garage sales or flea markets selling the same item? If there are more supplies, then the demand is lower; hence, the price is lower too.

Take note that how important or memorable the item to you does not count. The customer would not really care if it were your baby's first toy or book. So, do not include the sentimental value of the item when you are doing the pricing.

Here are several tips to do when pricing your items.

Do your research. First, do some research in your neighborhood. Before your scheduled garage sale starts, check items that are similar to yours and take note of everything so you won't end up pricing your items too high. Because people will normally haggle, setting a low price right off the bat is definitely among the biggest mistakes you could possibly make. Aside from checking other items' prices (and quality), make it a point to talk with the experts. For example, if you're going to sell vintage videogames, it'd be necessary to have someone knowledgeable in such things appraise your goods.

If you don't personally know anyone who could help you in those matters, remember that there are groups of people dedicated to all kinds of hobbies. Let's say you're trying to determine the price of an action figure from the early 90s, you could look for groups of toy collectors that often meet (or have their headquarters) near your place. Since many of those groups have their own websites, finding their exact location shouldn't be that hard. Of course, politely asking information from just one member could be enough.

If conversing with local "experts" isn't an option, you could go the online route. There are many discussion boards that focus on very specific collections. While there's some Googling required to succeed in this endeavor, rest assured that joining a relevant discussion board will get you answers. True collectors or enthusiasts are always more than eager to help those less knowledgeable – so long as questions are asked politely and forum rules are followed. Of course, it wouldn't be surprising if you immediately get offers for your items.

Those who truly wish to be thorough in their price-identification adventure should also visit as many local pawnshops as possible. Why is there a need to visit several pawnshops? Well, it's not that unlikely for some pawnshop owners to try to rip off potential sellers, feeding them false information.

Visit specialty community boards online and ask around about how much an item could be worth. This is especially the case with antiques and collectibles.

Use The Golden Rule For Garage Sale Pricing.
If you do not have time to do research (which is highly
recommendable that you do), you can use the short
cut and do your pricing according to the golden rule of
yard sale pricing. What is it? Ask yourself this
question – If I am the buyer and I want or need to buy
this, how much would I be willing to pay for it?

Putting yourself on the shoes of the buyer is the trick.
Why? Simple. Doing to others what you want others
to do to you (which is the original golden rule) is
proven to work each time. You do not want to be
ripped off right? Then do the same to your customers.
After all, having garage sales is not a single time event
in your life. You would have other garage sales in the
future. You are establishing your integrity. These
clients would become loyal patrons when you set the
price where both of you would be happy and satisfied.
Another thing to remember with this rule is that the
buyer has no sentimental attachment to the item.
Therefore, when deciding how much to price an item,
be objective and remove the emotions you have for the
item. In the absence of how you feel about a particular
item, would you pay for it at this price? If the answer
is yes, then simply add another 25% to 50% on it
(since you know that the would-be customer would
haggle and try to negotiate). If the answer is no, then

lower the price to what you think is reasonable. Add the mark-up and place the price tag on the item.

Another Yard Sale Pricing Strategy – the 10% Rule. Check the current retail price of the item and mark your prices at 10%. So if the item costs $100, the bottom line price (this is the lowest price you are willing to take for the item) is $10. The price on the tag should be between $12.5-15 (add 25-50% to the bottom line price, remember?). Again, this is to provide "room to move the price" when negotiations start.

Most garage sale holders use the 20% or 30% pricing strategy instead of the 10% rule. Be careful though, as this could turn off clients. Your items have no warranties or guarantees at all so they would definitely have second thoughts in buying if they feel that the items were highly priced.

Label items clearly and individually. Placing a sign which say "Everything is $1" at one table and "Everything is $5" at another table might be easier for you but it could result in chaos and more work later on. How? A customer might accidentally (or intentionally) get an item from the $5 table and claim it to be from the $1 table. Or a client might return a $5 item to the $1 table. Or can you imagine adding up 10 items both from the $1 and $5 tables? That could be confusing, right?

Labeling items individually might mean extra work for you now but it would save you energy and time during the actual selling. Plus, it could also avoid mix-ups of prices.

You can buy price stickers at your local convenience store. Place those directly on your items (this isn't always an option though, as stickers tend to leave marks on some objects) or anywhere easily seen by visitors. This advise is for people who don't want to be bombarded with "How much for this one?" questions. But if you don't mind talking to the customers, then you can make your prices as you go along the whole process, talking it through with potential buyers.

You could also do your own tie-on tags. Simply cut bright colored poster papers into different shapes (stars, hearts, squares, and other shapes). Use a small puncher to make a hole. Thread a string through the hole or use rubber bands. Write down the price and attach to your item. For some reasons, people find items with tie-on tags more appealing than stickers so this might do the trick of selling your items.

Prevent swapping of tie-on tags. The disadvantage of tie-on tags is that some customers might try to outsmart you and do swapping of tie-on tags. You can protect yourself by including a code or a short description on the price tag. When they hand you the item, check if the price tag and item match according to your code.

Perform a Price Comparison. For high-priced items, this strategy is effective. If it is the same or almost similar item as yours, then simply cut out the ad of the item in catalogue and attach it to your item or price tag. That way, the potential buyers would be able to compare the price and of course, appreciate the discount they will get from you. If there is no catalogue, you can do your own research. Put the current price and other information of the similar item on an index card and then place it beside the price tag of your item.

Have an inventory list. Feel free to develop your own system, especially if not all items are yours. If that's the case, you better keep a logbook with you, listing which items are sold the whole time your sale is open. At the end of the day, you should talk to the people involved in the sale and have them identify which items were theirs. By this method, you could easily track who made a sale and give him or her money accordingly. (Of course, this is applicable only if very few items aren't yours; if other people also have a lot of things to sell, it'd be better to simply have separate logbooks – as previously suggested.)

Be a good haggler. Rule of thumb dictates that always raise the price of your goods a little. This is just to prepare you for future negotiations because whatever you do (even if you put a price tag on your items individually), people will always look for a better deal. The seller and the buyer should both be satisfied with their transactions, with the favor skewing a little bit towards the seller. They won't care if those shoes were worn by a famous athlete and his or her stench still seeps out of it—at the end of the day, people will opt for a good deal; that's what they came for anyway. So, overprice but don't be greedy. Put yourself in the customer's shoes and imagine getting ripped off. It doesn't feel good, does it?

Haggling and negotiating will be further discussed in the succeeding chapters.
Other Things to Remember:
- Picture frames will only be valuable and sell well if they're unique.
- Stuffed toys or animals are so-so sellers.
- Different forms of art (like paintings) will always be tricky to sell. The marketability of paintings is very subjective that making a solid deal is difficult. You have to be at the right place at the right time, talking with the right person. If you

still have plenty of room in your sale, you could include such works of art. If you do try to sell artwork, make sure that the frames you're going to use are presentable.

- Be honest about your items. If you're trying to sell a bed and you'd like to avoid questions, place notes on it saying things like how it is or whether it'll come with pillows, blankets, and sheets. This can also be done if you're selling electronics such as TVs. You can add a note saying, "Working TV $8—broken left speaker".

Chapter 4

Advertising and Layout

"Garage Sale" Signs

What good is having a garage sale when not a single soul knows about it? You can have all the treasures in the world to share but if no one even knows you exist, all the hard work will go down the drain. The next thing you should do now is to find a way to advertise your sale.

First, ask your local authority if your city has a sign display policy. Some cities have many restrictions when it comes to putting up a sign. Examples include the allowable size of the sign, where you can place your sign, and how many signs each seller is allowed to post.

If you have kids or little nephews and nieces that want to help out, this is their time to shine. Or if you have that friend who's just playing with the items on sale, tell him he's now tasked with something very important. Ask him to make a simple sign that says, "Garage Sale" (it's perfectly fine to give the event another name, but never forget to indicate that it's a garage sale). Remind whoever is going to make the sign that it doesn't need to be very colorful; adding lots of glitter isn't necessary as well. In this case, just bold, big, and simple lettering will do the trick. You may also include an arrow sign pointing towards your location.

Remember to be a considerate and law abiding citizen; ask permission before you staple or nail your signs or flyers. Go to your local authority or homeowners association and ask about the designated areas where you're allowed to post your signs or flyers so you can appropriately post your sign(s), leading the people to your sale.

Local Newspaper Ad

You can also contact your local newspaper and try to put an ad for your upcoming garage sale. Some companies have yard sales/garage sales under their classified ads so don't hesitate and put your sale on the map. Don't forget to include the date, time, and the address where your sale will take place. To really get some attention on your sale, you can also list down your categories to pique the interest of serious potential buyers.

Advertise Online

With how technology works nowadays, you should take full advantage of it. Use different social networking sites (like Facebook and Twitter) to get your sale out there. It will also help to post pictures, descriptions of the items, and regular updates prior to the actual day of opening to build excitement. You'll be surprised how diverse your clients will be, so you better use your resources effectively.

Also check free classified-ads websites (like craigslist.com, USFreeAds.com, Kudzu.com, iNetGiant.com, iPost360.com, DomesticSale.com, and Classifieds.Yahoo.com) to post your advertisement for free. Advertising through websites is definitely effective. You should post your advertisement a week before the sale then re-post the ad every other day. Include specific details of your items such as brands, sizes, and colors.

So, when people search for stuff on these websites, your items will show up in the search results page. Just be sure to post items that are known hot sellers. The more specific your descriptions about your items, the better your sales will be.

Chapter 5

Designing the Overall Garage Sale Layout

Whether you like it or not, presentation is important. You have done the preparations, items all checked out, and your garage sale dates are now known all over the web—the next thing to do is make your sale presentable. The way you offer your items reflect a little bit about your personality, so make sure your customers won't have a bad impression (otherwise, they'll simply choose to walk past your sale).

Keep these things in mind when setting up your garage sale layout. The client should be able to:

- Go through all the items in an unhurried manner.
- See and touch all your items.
- Feel comfortable while looking around.
- Be safe.
- Feel compelled to buy.

First off, set up tables in a way that all small and medium-sized items remain perfectly visible. If you don't have a lot of tables, borrow a few from friends or neighbors; you could also opt to rent additional tables, but that entails the need to spend a little bit of money.

For clothes, it's better to have a clothesline to hang them to (old or new) so people can see their choices immediately. As mentioned beforehand, folding clothes isn't that smart, particularly if you're expecting to see dozens of customers rummaging through your goods.

If you have big furniture or large items, it's good to have them somewhere in front of your sale, so it is easy to move them out when these items get sold. You can also use those as a way of getting the attention of a casual passerby, placing something cool and authentic in your driveway or somewhere near the curb to make them check out your sale. Maybe you can attach balloons or something; it's up to you.

As much as possible, do not place boxes (with your items for sale) on the ground. Most people cannot bend for long. Plus, it is more difficult to rummage through the box. Items on the bottom of the box are prone to be overlooked or totally forgotten.

To make it easier, pretend like you have a shop for the day or for the weekend. What does a department store look like? Does it have food and nail polish in the same pile? Treat it as a legitimate store and see everything from a customer's point of view.

Safety is a Priority. As long as they are within your premises, they are your responsibilities. Plan ahead and imagine how it would be with children and parents around. Also, protect your items so that they will not be damaged. Here are some things you can do:

- Place fragile and breakable items near the back of each table. In this place, they will not be knocked off easily plus they would be out of reach of children. Also, display the price tag in front so that the client would not need to touch the item to see the price unless he is really interested in checking and buying the item.
- Make sure each table's legs are sturdy enough to support the weight of the items.
- Remove cords and other objects that can trip the clients especially their little children.
- Have an emergency first aid kit.

Other Things to Remember:

- If you're not certain about the weather, have some shade prepared just in case.
- This is optional but during summer, your customers might get restless or thirsty from the warm temperature. So, you could have your kid set up a lemonade stand or ask your friends to offer some refreshments. It's a good way to have a good relationship with the people. Of course,

it's up to if you want to offer refreshments free of charge.

- Clean your garage!
  - o Trim the grass in your yard if you ever decide to hold your sale outside.
  - o Dust off items.
  - o Place curtains or blankets on the shelves or items in your garage that are not included in the sale. This will keep prying customers from handling your things that are not for sale.
- Don't place books and beauty products (they can melt) under direct sunlight.
- See to it that you can still move around the place comfortably; sufficient space matters not only to you but also to your customers.
- Have a testing station (especially for CDs, DVDs, electronics, and other similar goods) for customers' peace of mind.
- Arrange the jewelry pieces in an organized manner.
  - o Secure the pairs of earrings in a zip lock plastic.
  - o You can also hang the earrings and necklaces on a corkboard so that they will not appear disorganized. That would also prevent them from getting tangled.

- o Have a mirror ready. The clients would want to try the jewelry and see how they look on her or him before buying them.
- o Use the board of the long tissue roll and place the bracelets there.

With the advertising and garage layout done, you are now ready for the big day.

Chapter 6.

What To Do On The Night Before And The Morning Of Your Garage Sale?

Preparation is key to a successful, organized, peaceful, enjoyable and of course, profitable garage sale day. Make the event smooth by doing all you can the night before the actual garage sale day. The morning of the sale is not the time to look for pens or extension cords. That could be stressful both for you and your clients.

Preparations on the night before the sale:
- If the area is covered and secured, you could start arranging the tables, boxes and items. If not, you and your helpers should be an hour or two early in the morning to arrange the set up.
- As you place the items on the tables, double check if there is a price tag on each of them.
- If you would set up Lemonade stand, place the cans of sodas and drinks on the fridge to cool them overnight.
- Prepare your meals for the whole day. There might not be time to cook. You could just heat the food the next day.
- Ready the small bills and loose change.

- Tape the cords down. That would prevent any person from tripping.
- Prepare the signage, decorations, scissors, measuring tape, masking tapes, calculator, first aid kit, and other items you would need during the sale.
- Charge all cellphones and gadgets.
- Get a lot of rest and sleep. You would need the extra energy for the next day.

Preparations on the morning of the sale:

This is the big day. It would also be a busy day. Make sure that you and your helpers have a heavy breakfast. Be positive. Expect it to be a great day for you.

If your ads reached a number of people, it's possible that you might receive calls or have people coming over to your house possibly days or hours before your sale officially opens. These people are called "early birds". Early birds are those looking to find a deal before anything else happens.

Don't worry though; you don't have to feel obligated to entertain them. You can politely send them away and wait for the actual opening time. If you feel bad doing so, again don't worry. These are dedicated garage sale shoppers and if you send them off nicely, they will definitely be back come opening time.

It's no secret that conducting a garage sale can and will promote a friendly vibe in your neighborhood but sadly there are people who will take advantage of this. Make sure to lock every door in your house, including that of the basement (if you have one). Rope off private areas. Set boundaries around your sale so customers won't wander aimlessly around your property. The people who are lending you a hand should also be vigilant if ever slight problems occur.

Now you are almost ready. Wear the belt bag (with the small bills and loose change), get your notebook and pen, and be ready with your smile. When the tables, decorations, and items are ready, display the street sign outside to signal the start of the garage sale.

Play some music, and if you want to go for a relaxing atmosphere, you could also light some scented candles. These are effective ways of calming the nerves of both the buyers and the sellers. At this time, you can also set up the Lemonade stand.

Now you are ready to welcome your clients and guests. Keep an enthusiastic and a positive attitude. When the clients come pouring in, be ready. Make them feel comfortable.

How to keep people coming to your garage sale? Make sure that the front of your display is attractive so that passers-by would be tempted to stop and browse around. Call friends, especially those who are interested in your items and remind them of the garage sale. Take good care of your clients, as they are the best advertisement that you can have. If they had an enjoyable experience, they are bound to tell 3 to 4 friends or family members. However, if they had an awful experience, be aware that they would tell 10 of their friends. That could hurt your sales. Therefore, try to be nice to everybody.

Tidy your table. Refill the tables with other items once sales are made. Well-stocked tables would attract more clients. If you are not too busy, you can re-arrange the items as you see fit. Maybe the hard to sell items can be paired with other in demand items. That way, you are effectively disposing the unsellable items and at the same time, you are getting a good price for the sellable items.

All throughout the day make your garage sale looks busy. If you are with friends or helpers, encourage them to look over the items as though they are clients. That would encourage potential clients to visit your garage sale. If they would see all of you just seated in one corner, they might hesitate to enter. If you are by yourself, be busy and fuss over your table. That will give the impression that something is happening at your garage sale. Do this rather than sit on the corner and wait for clients to come.

Chapter 7

The Big Day: The Actual Sales and Negotiation

It's show time! Keep that smile on your face and be ready to welcome and entertain your clients and make some money. In addition, here are other important things you have to keep in mind all throughout the big day.

Be an active seller. Your items will not sell by themselves, that's for sure. After you have acknowledged and welcomed your clients, allow them time to roam and look at the items. There is no need to hover over them. Most of them feel uncomfortable when you do that. Just be approachable and ready in case they need assistance. You can show off your items and enumerate their good qualities if your client shows interest in them.

"Keep an eye on the customers". Real buyers and unfortunately, shoplifters, go to garage sales. It is important that you are alert all the time. Be ready for anything. If something feels out of place, trust your gut feeling and be more cautious and attentive. Instruct your helpers to do the same. Treat each client

nicely but carefully. You can never really tell just by their looks if they are genuine or fakes.

Decide ahead if you are going to let the clients use your bathroom or not. If you do allow them, make sure that all the other rooms are locked. The best thing to do is to ask a helper to accompany the client to the bathroom and wait for the client and bring him/her back to the garage sale area. If you would not allow them to use your bathroom, point them to a nearby gas station, fast food store or convenience shop.

Secure the money at all times. What better way to do this than wear a money belt? It may not look stylish but with you is the safest place for the money. Putting the money in a small safe box is sometimes not safe. Someone could pick it up very quickly and be gone in seconds. There should be only one to handle the money. Accounting after the day will be easier plus there is no room for confusion on the part of the client where to pay or who to look for. Get all the price tags or stickers, or if that is not possible, record all the sales for the day.

Say out loud (for other people to hear) how much you receive from the client. For example, say "I received $20." Do not put the money in the belt bag until after you have given the change and the client has accepted it as correct. These are strategies to avoid "the client's word against your word" conflict on how much money he/she issued you. There are many records where the client would insist that he has handed a $100 bill or other bills.

This is also why you should have small bills and loose change ready. If you do not have them, you would be forced to go and look while your client waits. A lot can happen between that time, including your client forgetting how much he has given you. The quicker the payment scheme, the better it is for you.

Be organized. There should be a flow of how sales should be conducted. For instance, when the sale is closed and payment has been made, do you have plastic bags ready to place the bought items? Do you have old newspapers to wrap the fragile or breakable items? If the dresser were sold, who would help the client put it in his car? Think ahead of all the possible scenarios and you must have a plan of action to take. Have a contingency plan too in case the first plan is not feasible.

Dress appropriately. So what should you be wearing on the big day itself? It might seem odd but the proper attire is something not so extravagant. Looking your best would send a message that you do not need the money and the clients would try to pressure you to lower your prices. However, make sure that you are tidy and pleasant to look at. Nobody would also like to deal with someone who looks sloppy.

Accident-proof the area. Your property is your responsibility, right? The same thing applies for people who are in your property. They are your responsibility, too. Secure the premises and make it accident-proof.

The most common cause of accident is slips and falls (usually by little kids or elderly clients). Make sure that there is nothing that can cause them to trip. Secure all the cords and cables on the floor by taping them down and getting them out of the way, as much as possible. Plus, keep the floor dry at all times. When a glass of lemonade or soda is spilled, put a signage that the floor is wet and immediately wipe it dry.

Sharp objects should be out of reach of children plus putting a note that the object is really sharp is also another way of keeping you and the client safe.

Constantly rearrange the set up of the store. Sold items put money on the money belt but leave the table bare. Those empty spaces on the table can ruin your presentation. Replace items quickly so that your tables would always look well stocked. You can also remove a table and combine the items on the remaining tables.

Upsell, upsell, upsell. This is a sales technique where you would encourage the client to purchase add-ons or other items related to his previous purchase. The client must not feel pressured however. Simply casually mention or show him the other items. For instance, after a client bought the blender, maybe he would also be interested in the margarita glasses.

Have fun. This is really important plus contagious. If they can see you are enjoying yourself, the clients would, too. Always keep that welcoming smile and positive attitude. It would brush off to other people as well.

The Art of Negotiation
All you need to know about negotiation is it's a challenging but wonderful dance. As a seller, you aim to establish good relationships with your customers without pressuring them or making them feel uncomfortable. Start with some small talk and don't go yapping about how awesome your prices are. You may not know it but some people just go to garage sales for the opportunity to meet interesting people and probably to share information about the products you have.

Always be nice to your customers. If you see a rather large gentleman looking through clothes clearly too small for his size, don't glare or make snappy comments. In case you don't know, he might be shopping for his kids or maybe, a friend asked him to look for something specifically.

Don't be afraid to make a deal. Most likely, some of your customers have experience in haggling. A bundle, most of the time, is very enticing. Still, you'll have to check if both you and the buyer will have a sweet deal. There are times that a customer will come to you carrying a huge haul, offering a small amount for it.

If you decline, you probably will see the customer returning the items one-by-one; don't get discouraged and propose another deal—this time to your advantage. Eventually, understand each other and try to be on the same page. However, if the customer keeps insisting and you're really not satisfied with the deal, the smartest thing to do is to forget about that deal and wait for a better one. The one who will be satisfied is always the person who has the ability to reject an offer.

Maintain the positive atmosphere whether the sale is doing good or not. Most of the time, there is a last minute mini-rush. These are the clients who are expecting more discounts as you are about to end the garage sale. Sometimes, this is when money comes pouring in. So do not be disheartened if the sale seems slow during the day. It's not over until you close the garage sale.

Lastly, have you considered any plans on what to do with all the items that won't be sold? There are organizations that will appreciate any form of help particularly donations.

Chapter 8
What To Do After The Garage Sale

Congratulations! Your endeavor is *almost* over. Take note that all garage sales, even the most successful ones, do not sell everything. There would always be "leftovers". So do not be dismayed that after all the hard work, you still have several boxes left with you with just an hour or two to go before the closing of the sale.

Here are strategies you can take to lessen the leftovers with 1-2 hours to spare.

Have a huge price slash. Decide on the lowest possible price that you are willing to give for your items. Make a huge sign of the price slash both inside and outside the area. You can also call those interested clients who wanted to buy those items at lower prices earlier. Inform them of the "sale" within the sale.

Free-for-all offer. If you have no intention of bringing those items back inside your house, announce a free-for-all deal. Anybody can take the items they want on the specific table that you allotted for that. You can do this systematically by asking them to fall in love and just fill one plastic bag each. Ensure that you have not left valuable items there. It's amazing how easily your items would vanish by doing this.

Other details

Another thing to expect before the closing time is the surge of crowd. This is quite common as many clients know that price slash occurs near the closing time. They are aware that at this time, all you want is to get rid of the remaining items hence they can expect better deals. Plus, at this time, you are expectedly tired and have less energy to negotiate.

When you are already close, do not be surprise when this occurs also - latecomers. There would always be shoppers who would be there when you have removed the signs or even closed your garage. You may be tempted to extend your time for latecomers but remember, after the garage sale, there are tons of activities to do. Are you willing to add more hours after just to entertain these potential buyers? If not, then politely tell them that the garage sale is over and you are now close. You need to allot time for cleaning, clearing and accounting.

Planning includes the activities to do after the garage sale. Here is the checklist of things-to-do after the garage sale.

1. ***Take down all the signs and flyers***. You must collect all the printed advertisement that you posted. Plus, do not forget to update your online advertisements too.

2. ***Pack up***. Clear all the tables and put all the items in boxes. You can do the following:

    a. ***Segregate***. Prepare three big boxes for the leftovers. Place all the items you are willing to take back in and resell in your next garage sale in the first box. The second box is for charity. Think of all the possible recipients who would be happy to get all those items for free. For instance, your doctor or dentist would love to have those magazines. Or maybe the leftover toys and baby books would be useful to the church or day care nearby. The third box is for all the items that you really do not want inside your house. Maybe, it's time to let these items go.

    b. ***Let them go***. So you do not want them and nobody else want those items, too. Maybe it is time to say goodbye to them permanently. After you have decided that nobody would really benefit by having them, throw them away in the trash bin. That would keep the dust off your house plus you would have that space that you badly need. Remember to dispose wastes properly and legally.

3. ***Compute the earnings***. Simply count the sales of the day and then subtract all your expenses (cost of signage, helpers, stickers, permits, taxes, and other miscellaneous items). The result is the profit or gain.

4. ***Evaluate the event***. This is important as the success of the next garage sale depends on this. Yes, there will be a next garage sale. There always is as you can get hooked to this. Be objective and see:

    a. What are the things you did right?
    b. What are the things you need to improve?
    c. What are the things you should never, ever do again in your next garage sale?

    You could also ask your friends and helpers to evaluate the event.

5. ***Learn from the garage sale***. You have discovered that you have so many items in the house that are not really important or useful for you. The next time you are tempted to buy a luxurious item, think twice. Are you really going to use it or are just going to place it in the garage sale next summer? Compute the potential losses that you may incur for buying items that you would just convince others to buy with 90% off the current price six months after the purchase. Be a wise shopper.

6. ***Reclaim the garage, attic and basement***.
   You have removed many items from these rooms
   and now you have adequate space again. This is
   not the sign that you need to buy items again to
   fill these places once more. On the contrary, this
   is the time to let these rooms be used for the very
   purpose they are made. Or, at least convert them
   into more useful ones. Your attic can house the
   truly precious items that you want to keep. The
   basement can be your teen's new room or maybe
   music room (to keep the neighbors from
   complaining) or it can also be your new
   recreational room for the whole family. The
   garage, well for a change, let the cars be parked
   there now.

When done right, having a garage sale is one
profitable, fun and memorable event in you and your
family's life. Have stress-free, easy and enjoyable
garage sales when you follow the tips and suggestions
given in this book. Good luck!

Conclusion

Thank you again for downloading this book!

I hope this book was able to help you to plan, hold, and have fun with your garage sale.

The next step is to put all these steps into action.

Finally, if you enjoyed this book, please take the time to share your thoughts and post a review on Amazon. It'd be greatly appreciated!
Thank you and good luck!

Made in the USA
Las Vegas, NV
01 May 2025

21596076R00036